AF000465

THOUGHTS AND MEMORIES OF MY LIFE OF ILLNESS AND MY LONGING FOR THE ETERNAL HOMELAND

ANNA SCHÄFFER

THOUGHTS AND MEMORIES OF MY LIFE OF ILLNESS AND MY LONGING FOR THE ETERNAL HOMELAND

Edited by
Georg Franz X. Schwager

SCHNELL + STEINER

The original of the writings of Anna Schäffer (*Thoughts and Memories of my Life of Illness – and My Longing for the Eternal Homeland!*) can be found in the Diocesan Consistory of Regensburg, Department for the Causes of Saints and Blessed, (Anna Schäffer Cause) K 12a XII.

With ecclesiastical approval
Mons. Michael Fuchs, Vicar General
Regensburg, 16.01.2012

Reproduction of the text is authorized only with specific acknowledgement of the source. **Photo reproduction** granted only with the express authorization of the Diocesan Consistory of Regensburg.

Bibliographic information published by the Deutsche Nationalbibliothek
The Deutsche Nationalbibliothek lists this publication in the Deutsche Nationalbibliografie; detailed bibliographic data are available in the Internet at http://dnb.dnb.de .

1. Edition 2012
© 2012 Verlag Schnell & Steiner GmbH,
Leibnizstr. 13, D-93055 Regensburg
Translation: Sr. Nancy Celaschi, OSF
Printing: Erhardi Druck GmbH, Regensburg
Cover Design: Anna Braungart, Tübingen
ISBN 978-3-7954-2624-8

All rights reserved. Electronic or photomechanical production of this book or excerpts thereof is prohibited without the express permission of the publisher and the Diocesan Consistory of Regensburg.

Additional information about the publisher can be found at
www.schnell-und-steiner.de

Contents

Introduction

In an undated, lined school notebook Anna Schäffer left behind her handwritten thoughts and memories of her life of illness and – as she herself expressed it – her longing for the eternal homeland. In these notes she opens up her heart and offers the attentive reader a glimpse of her rich interior life, a life formed by the cross of Jesus Christ and nourished by the divine Sacrament of the Most Holy Eucharist. Some of the thoughts jotted down here are also found scattered throughout Anna Schäffer's letters[1]. In writing her memoirs however, it seems as if she wanted in some way to leave a compilation of her spiritual life. Given the significance of these notes, it is reasonable to assume it fitting to publish them in a single volume.

Anna Schäffer had no intention of presenting a systematic study of her interior life; as the pen strokes of the manuscript show, she put her thoughts and memories on paper over a long period of time. In

1 See "Im Leiden habe ich Dich lieben gelernt! Die Schriften Anna Schäffers" (*In suffering have I learned to love you! The writings of Anna Schäffer.*) Documented by Emmeram H. Ritter, Regensburg 1999.

them she gives us a genuine witness of her hidden love for Christ. In many places her notes give the reader the impression that they are more like a prayer, her intimate conversations with the Lord, to which at times she inserts traditional prayers or well-known ejaculations.

Through these notes Anna Schäffer comes to speak of the sources from which she drew the strength needed to form her interior life, to bear her suffering and to expiate for the sins of others: the gaze of the Crucified and the love of the cross as a pledge of redemption; the reception of Holy Communion as a daily encounter with Christ; her meditative recitation of the Rosary, which she was wont to refer to as her "game of roses" and the "faithful friend by my sickbed", to mention but a few of the more important sources. It is to them that Anna's spiritual formation can be attributed. However, she composed her writings out of obedience, as she herself acknowledges: "In holy obedience I wrote, and I gladly continue to fill, these notebooks"[2]. We owe these letters and most certainly this volume to this attitude of hers.

External form and dating of the original manuscript

The original of Anna Schäffer's *Thoughts and Memories of My Life of Illness – and My Longing for the Heavenly Homeland* is held in the archives of the Department for Beatification and Canonization Processes in the Diocesan Consistory of Regensburg[3]. As noted above, it consists of a lined school notebook (4a lineation; 21 cm in height and 16,5 cm in width) and covers 26 pages filled in notes written in blue ink in a cramped but quite legible German script. Ten pages of the notebook are empty. Between the individual thoughts Anna left a half-line or whole-line space. In the archive of the Department for Beatification and Canonization Processes there are also other transcriptions of the *Thoughts and Memories* of Anna documented here, a sign of the great esteem in which this work is held. At the end of one of these transcriptions[4] there is a short passage which was obviously added later. In this volume it is published in square brackets [ ] and set in italic type to distinguish it from the rest. Perhaps Anna dictated these passages from her sickbed as a supplement, probably while she was in the last stages of her life and no longer capable of writing letters by her own hand.

As for the question of the dating of Anna Schäffer's original manuscript, we can consider the following: in her remembrances Anna speaks of a suffering that has already lasted for 21 years. Literally, she wrote: "My suffering has lasted for more than 21 years. Daily I experience to some degree the nails of the cross and the points of the crown of thorns."[5] Since her tragic accident took place on 4 February 1901 in Stammham near Mindelstetten[6], the time frame for the text is at most sometime between the years 1922 and 1925 (Anna died in the evening of 5 October 1925). It should also be noted that Anna's health deteriorated from 1923 onwards[7]. In her last years she was afflicted with immeasurable pain throughout

2 Anna Schäffer, Letter of 3 July 1919, in: BKR Abt. C.A.S. Proc. sup. perqu. Scriptorum D. 44–76 K. 10.

3 BKR Abt. C.A.S. Proc. sup. perqu. Scriptorum D. I–XIII K. 12 a, AS 12.

4 BKR Abt. C.A.S. „Abschriften: Gedanken u. Erinnerungen / Traum-Buch / Gedichte / Tatsachenberichte über AS" K. 16, AS 19.

5 See p. 50 of this documentation.

6 Cf. Andrea Ambrosi, "Informatio super virtutibus", in: *Congregatio de Causis Sanctorum P. N. 1354 – Ratisbonensis Canonizationis Servae Dei Annae Schäffer iuvenis saecularis (1882–1925) Positio super virtutibus, Roma* 1992, p. 27.

7 Cf. ibid, p. 40.

her whole body, with seeping wounds and cramps throughout her nervous system[8]. These considerations allow us place the composition of her thoughts and memories closer to the years 1922 and 1923. Since Anna herself did not date her notes, it is impossible for us to be more precise.

Organization and structure

The thoughts and memories of Anna Schäffer about her life of illness reveal the structure the author herself gave it. Anna begins her notes with the heading, "God alone, God alone suffices!" This dedication alsoserves to reveal her conviction. The reader will spontaneously think of the famous saying of St. Teresa of Avila (1515–1582) from one of her poems: "Let nothing disturb you, Let nothing frighten you, All things pass away: God never changes. Patience obtains all things. He who has God finds he lacks nothing"[9]. Anna's thoughts and memories follow, as has already been mentioned, written quite legibly and structured in short sections. Anna adds to this first part of her notes thoughts and considerations for the twelve months of the year. The reader immediately notices that she begins all twelve months with a short prayer to the Blessed Virgin Mary, thus entrusting herself to Mary's special protection and blessing, greeting her with titles referring to events or mysteries celebrated that month. Thus, for example, in the month of February mindful of the beginning of Lent, she calls her the "Mother of Sorrows", in May she invokes the "Queen of May", in October "Queen of the Rosary", and in December the "Immaculate Conception". Anna Schäffer concludes this section with a verse prayer and an offering of the Body and Blood of Christ to the

Heavenly Father through Mary's hands for those who were dying that day. This is followed by a poem (with its own title) to her guardian angel, followed again by thoughts and recommendations, which she offers the reader from the experience of her life with illness. The last part of the texts is composed of Anna's "Daily offering of my 12 hours of reparation before the Most Blessed Sacrament!", an evening examination of conscience" and a 14-line spiritual epilogue entitled, "Jesus is my Life – Death my Gain!", which concludes Anna's *Thoughts and Memories* with the quite beautiful ejaculation often found in her letters, "My God, I thank You! – My God, I love you!"

Spiritual objective

Where does Anna Schäffer want to lead the reader of her notes? She herself gives us a response when she completed the title of her Thoughts and Memories with the words "... and my longing for the eternal homeland". Anna longs for the happiness of heaven where her suffering and cross will lead her, where "Christ is seated at the right hand of the Father" (Col 3: 1). The Christian life is a life "hidden with Christ in God" (Col 3:3). Anna's life too was hidden from

---

8 Cf. Letter of 12 January 1904 from Father Carl Rieger to Frau Gruber in Zurich, in: BKR Abt. C.A.S. Akten 1921–1925 K. 19.

9 Cf. Schott, Messbuch für die Wochentage (*Weekday Missal*). Teil II. 14. bis 34. Woche im Jahreskreis (Part II, 14th to 34th weeks in Ordinary Time), Freiburg im Breisgau 1984, p. 1447; „Gott allein genügt – Dios solo basta" ("God alone suffices") Geistliches Wort (A spiritual reflection.) Sister Gemma Hinricher OCD, in: www.karmelberlin.de

the world's eyes, but through her union with Christ it was sheltered in God and his love. She wanted to be one with him. Thus she could write: "How easy it is to die with Jesus on the cross – if one has lived with Jesus on the cross!"[10] She prays that her whole life may be a quiet, hidden life on the cross, that she may bloom as a "passion flower"[11] at the foot of the holy Cross, hidden to the world but some day shining bright in the light of God's light in eternity.

Near the end of her manuscript Anna cites the famous passage from the Apostle St. Paul: "I no longer live, not I, but Christ lives in me" (cf. Gal 2: 20)[12]. In her decades-long suffering, in her infirmity and her poverty she was, as if to say, crucified with Christ. He was, however, even more her life, nourished and strengthened by His Eucharistic Body. Countless times in her letters and even more apparent in her letters and in her *Thoughts and Memories of her Life of Illness* Anna Schäffer refers to the strengthening power of Holy Communion. With longing and love she prepares herself to receive the Eucharistic Lord and, in her own words, would like to "suffer martyrdom", with the sole intention that Jesus in the Eucharistic Sacrament would be better known and loved.[13].

Thus from her sickbed Anna achieved the height and perfection of Christian living. She found her purpose in conformity to Christ and in becoming one with him. Anna Schäffer achieved her goal by taking up her personal cross and accepting her suffering in a spirit of penance in expiation for sins, guided by the Eucharistic Lord and His grace. May Anna Schäffer's *Thoughts and Memories* become a valuable companion for all its readers, and especially for all her many devotés. With her and like her, may all of them be gifted with a holy life and a dying filled with longing for the eternal homeland. May the most Blessed Virgin Mary, Mother of God and Queen of All Saints, who herself remained in suffering and fidelity beneath the cross of Jesus, be their intercessor.

Anna Schäffer began her notes with the saying, "God alone suffices!"God alone truly suffices. Only in God is every person safe and secure in joy, even amid life's sufferings. May God grant that the reading of and reflection on Anna Schäffer's *Thoughts and Memories* may linger in us as the prayer in which, at the end of her manuscript, she left us as a precious legacy and revealed to us the depths of her soul: "My God, I thank You! My God, I love you!"

Regensburg, 8 December 2011
(Solemnity of the Immaculate Conception of the Blessed Virgin Mary)

Msgr. Georg Schwager
Vicar of the Cathedral
Director of the Department
for Canonisation and Beatification
Processes of the Diocesan Consistory
of Regensburg

10 See p. 37 of this documentation.
11 See p. 30 of this documentation.
12 Cf. p. 57 of this documentation.
13 Cf. p. 31 of this documentation.

Thoughts and Memories of my Life of Illness – and my Longing for the Eternal Homeland!

God alone, God alone suffices!'

'Take up your cross and follow me!' These words from the *Imitation of Christ* with which the dear Saviour invites me to follow Him are the foundationstone of my heart in which the cross is set. With love and gratitude I will greet each moment – and in love of the cross and gratitude for the cross shall I draw my last life's breath!'

'On the cross – and in Holy Communion, O my Lord and God, have I learned to love you!'

'The cross must make God's will and the fullness of faith alive in our hearts so that each person can say of himself or herself: – I no longer live, – not I, – but Jesus the cross–bearer lives in me and with Him I go: following the cross!'

'The goal of my cross is: Calvary's height! I want to look upon this height whenever the painful stations of my life, my life of pain, my body is ploughed with pain. That light that comes streaming from on high – makes everything seem easy and light for me – because I see my model, my Saviour, and how much he has suffered for me, unworthy though I am. And united with Him, Whom I love and Who lives in my soul, I will gladly embrace my cross and follow Him: after the cross!'

The cross is the hammer – which fashions the eternal crown that we will wear in heaven, – if we have borne our cross with courage and resignation.

I have in my heart a quiet, holy joy because the Lord allows me to feel a little of the ardour of His cross.

The cross is my guide, – it is my strength, – it is my light, – it is my help, – it is my shield, – it is my comfort, – it is my shelter – it is my glory, – it is my pillar and it will be my reward!'

'When we look upon Jesus on the cross, – or consider His love in the Tabernacle, – we can bear everything patiently!'

'The cross and suffering, – they are my training for heaven!'

The way to heaven, – passes along the *via dolorosa* to Calvary, – and only from there towards the eternal dwelling places!

Through cross and suffering, affliction and unpleasantness, the Lord draws us towards His cross, towards the heights of Calvary. Only the one who follows Him to Calvary will accompany Him to the Mountain of His triumph, – because behind the suffering of this age, – lies the glory of God. Overcoming ourselves leads to the cross, – to the summit of love, – and that is why we renounce ourselves and follow the cross!'

I thirst, O Lord, for the cross and suffering and do not ask for another single drop of consolation in this valley of tears! Beneath the shadow of the cross and in the streaming light of the tabernacle I will spend my days of suffering. Every single drop of blood in the heart – Every sweet blast of pain – Every deep wound of suffering – Every sweet hour of joy – Everything for your honour, O God – To resound to your praise everywhere!'

It often seems that because of my pain I am entangled in a bed of thorns and I picture myself then as that little lamb that the Good Shepherd found among the brambles; then in the depths of my heart I have such holy joy that I know that the Lord is near me. Especially in this Lent since the pain is so often worse and I feel it, too...! Most Sacred Heart of Jesus, I thank You! I would like to lay every little rose of my suffering on the wounded heart of my heavenly Bridegroom, to console Him and make Him happy.

I will rejoice so much when I must leave this valley of tears. I shall be glad to go home, but not because I will be freed from my pain, but ...., but only (freed) for....! There too I would not like to be inactive for even a moment and I would gladly suffer until the end of time until all the sheep will have entered the great Sheepfold. My wish is, in heaven through my constant prayer, to be able to save so many sinful souls, which was also my only wish here below.

Now and in eternity, too, I would like to pray most of all for priests, especial for .... Because through the work of holy priests so many souls can be saved, so many souls reach perfection.

Hide me, O crucified Love, in the delightful wound of Your side, so that I can fall blissfully asleep and refresh myself in the slumber of Your honeysweet love!'

O my God, I love you, You, eternal Beauty, You Who always steal my heart whenever I think of You...!

'I thirst, O Lord, – satisfy me, O Fountain of Life! I thirst for Jesus in Holy Communion .... Oh, when can I finally go home in order to appear before the face of my God?

My eyes often fill with tears; and whenever I often lie all night long in the greatest of pain, I offer myself to my dear Jesus each time as a little reimbursement for the love and for the sins above all that have been committed against Him in the Blessed Sacrament.

O my Lord and Saviour, if you would sometimes gift me with a few hours of sleep, during this time I would also turn my heart to You, –– so that even in sleep I would be near You.

Through the cross and suffering, – I can hope in God's mercy!'

If someone would give me the choice between being completely healthy and enjoying every imaginable joy and not receiving Holy Communion; – or night and day experiencing the most bitter pain without sleeping and receiving Holy Communion every day – I would choose the latter, because all earthy suffering cannot compare with what I would have to bear in my heart if I had to do without Holy Communion.

United with Jesus .... I am happy every minute. And even when pain racks my body, in my heart I feel such bliss that I cannot even express it. This happiness, this bliss, that sweetens all my pain, I discovered on the most beautiful day of my life, at my First Holy Communion, when the eternal sunrise enlightened my heart... and every Holy Communion makes this fire so much bigger...! My God, I thank You! My God, I love you!

O my Jesus, the pain that I am feeling now I unite with Your pain and I will gladly bear it in reparation for my sins!'

'May the name of the Lord be ever magnified!'

My soul magnifies the Lord ....!

Whether I wake or sleep or suffer, I am peaceful and calm because my portion is the Lord, in whom I hope and trust ...!

Most Sacred Heart of Jesus, happy are all the souls who are consecrated to Your Heart in love and simplicity, – now and in eternity, You will be their abundant reward. Most Sacred Heart of Jesus, I trust in You and promise You to be good and to never do anything that I will ever regret!

Oh, – until now I have not been deemed worthy to go to the flowers that are eternally green and blooming, that surround Jesus alone. Mary, my Mother, lead me to Jesus ...!

Only through you, O my good Mother, can I reach Jesus.... Mother – turn your merciful eyes towards me and bind me eternally to the Heart of Jesus, glowing with love….!

Every morning brings the most wondrous feast of love to me…. when Jesus comes. So great is my longing for Holy Communion... or whenever in spirit I gaze upon the sacred Host in the Tabernacle...! My God, I love you ..!

Every heartbeat is for You – Dearest Saviour, bless me..!
Every pain is a relic for me…!
O cross of my Jesus, how dear and precious you are to me...!

God's will is enough for me and my will must completely die. This union with God's will lets me recognise in everything that suffering is my training for heaven. If with only one Hail Mary I could change my suffering (unless it were God's holy Will) I would not do it, because I love suffering with my dear Saviour and thus I always have a little something to offer Him in Holy Communion.

Whenever in spirit I gaze upon the sacred Host, everything else disappears.... I forget the suffering, and the hours that I spend before the Most Blessed Sacrament compensate for everything with their great happiness. I often feel as if I am being drawn by a mysterious power that often makes an entire night seem to me but only a few minutes. Oh satisfy my longing, – You, the Bridegroom of my soul – to receive You in spirit – You, the true sacrificial Lamb....! O hidden Lamb in the sacred Host, You are my one and my everything.... in You alone is my poor soul at rest..!

O Jesus, may my heart beat only with love for You. The entire offering of my life shall and must be: Love for love – for the dear Saviour. O dearest Jesus, You want me to love only what You are and what You love; – that I may be more mindful of mortifying myself, – than satisfying myself; – that I may treasure suffering more than joy; that I may produce good deeds, rather than nice sentiments; – that I may be more grateful to you for what is repugnant to me than for the consolations that I experience! That I prefer my neighbour's well-being over my own; – O Lord, in everything I want only your glory – and to seek you alone. My God, I love you!

Whenever the Lord abandons me in darkness of spirit, I hasten immediately to seek Him; even then I am extremely happy that I can in spirit feel and imitate that which I would prefer at any cost, even at the cost of my body, and that is to be hidden from and disdained , etc. in the eyes of the world. Even when in spirit I often have to travel many a dark path, – I grasp my little cross, in order to pass through the darkness more rapidly – and having sought Him hastily, contemplating the bitter suffering and death of Jesus, – I find him again on the Mount of Olives – or imprisoned in the Tabernacle.

Each day I also commend the poor souls of so many sinners to the Most Sacred Heart of Jesus and Mary in order to obtain their conversion...! During the celebration of the Holy Mass and at the Consecration each time I ask the dear Saviour for a drop of His Precious Blood for them...! At Holy Communion, I ask Him, to bind to his Heart burning with love all those for whom I pray. And I often pray thus with confidence and hope..! I entrust everything to the action of divine grace. The dear Saviour puts us to a difficult test and we must often pray for an awfully, awfully long time; and with God's grace knock for a long time on the door of the hearts of sinners, – until the sinner surrenders and allows grace to enter. The dear God waits until the sinner tires of walking the way of godlessness and then stops and thinks. One never prays in vain for a sinner, and the harder and deeper one prays for him, – the heavier will he feel the weight of his conscience, the more clearly he will recognise the paths of his sinfulness .... and all at once, grace opens the path to him and drives away from his heart the evil enemy, and all his sins and vices, – in the instant when in a repentant confession he places his heart open and clear before the Lord's representative. Most Sacred Heart of Jesus, give me many souls..... especially those... who can hardly help themselves any more because of despair. Most Sacred Heart of Jesus, increase my suffering .... And in return give me souls that I can save for You.

Mary, Refuge of Sinners, give me souls….

O Mary, my Mother – these words that speak so much to me are often carved on my heart and linger on my lips. Oh, my eyes are filling with tears, as I write this, … – because you, Mother of Mercy, Refuge of Sinners and the Comforter of the Suffering and the Afflicted, have already begged for countless graces for me. To you be thanks and love forever and ever. O Mary, my mother, lead me to Jesus! You alone know the longing of this poor heart for every Holy Communion.... and for heaven...! With every passing day I can say to myself: "one day closer to my longed-for goal!" O blessed dawn of eternity, you are welcome at every moment. Mary, my Morning Star and Evening Star. Mary is my guiding star in this valley of tears; I want to impress her virtues on my mind in order to imitate them and I want to be good and give her great joy, so that in her kindness and gentleness she may present me to her divine Son! Every word, O my dear mother, shall be consecrated to you. O Heavenly Mother, let me see you – when my heart stops beating!'

Every day I thank the dear Lord for having given me my intellect and preserving it so that I can thank Him for all my graces and suffering. Each breath shall be a prayer of thanksgiving and love and may I use each minute to advantage, especially during my many, many sleepless nights when I find great consolation in the time spent in contemplative prayer in spirit before the Blessed Sacrament. Oh how much I can say to the dear Saviour and console Him, atone for sins, etc. And then there's always the holy Rosary, which I so love to pray…., because through the recitation of the Rosary we obtain so much from our dear Saviour.....! My Rosary is my faithful companion all night long clutched in my hands often burning with the fire of my illness and by day too it is my "rose game" (as I often call it) whenever I am not knitting, writing, or doing anything else. Thus my rosary is often my true friend by my sickbed; – it teaches me to look upon and contemplate Jesus' life, passion, death and glory. It is the best preparation for Holy Communion; – it is my comforter during sleepless nights; in sorrow; – it is my guide towards the heavenly homeland and it is often my favourite form of conversation with Jesus and Mary. Queen of the Holy Rosary, pray for me...!

In preparation for and thanksgiving after Holy Communion, I do not always use a prayer book, but quite often I make up my own preparation and thanksgiving. Oh, how much I have to say to the dear Saviour, that is, to thank Him for His great love for me, a wretched sinner. Oh, how happy I am each time after Holy Communion....! I do not find anything in the prayer book as appropriate for praying to Jesus, thanking Him, etc. as when a person does so with the words of his own heart...! I have quite often thought that if I could remain alone and undisturbed after Holy Communion until late evening to speak with the dear Saviour, – it would, however, seem to me like only a minute. Oh, how I would love to pour out in words the ardour that fills me and penetrates my whole being,... and yet it has not been granted to me to describe.... because I can speak about it only with my heart. Oh, I would love to explain what I feel in those holy moments and what is in my heart, – and then I would be silent, because of the excess of my blessed feelings...!

O Sacrament, if only I could embrace you as I would like to – O sweet God, in my death – satisfy my longing....!

O dearest Jesus draw me to Yourself through a glimpse of Your beauty and Your infinite love that You reveal in the sacred Host ....!

O how I shall rejoice, when my days of suffering will come to an end, to go to Jesus forever...!

Only with God in love united – can true consolation be found!

O my dearest Jesus, I thank you for all the favours you have shown me! If it is Your holy will, increase my suffering so that I may soon enter into Your beatific vision!

The hard cross and suffering are my pride and joy.

Lord, teach me to pray, – Lord, teach me to love, – Lord, teach me to suffer...!

The dear God sows the cross and suffering – in order to grow the flowers of heaven!

Through the cross and suffering – to the joy of heaven!

After Holy Communion there are so many tender, holy moments, – that.... if they were exposed to the air.... They would immediately lose their sparkle..! In these moments one can only look at Jesus and love Him...!

If I yearn for a certain homily, I open up a chapter of the *Imitation of Christ*, – where every word in itself speaks to my soul and places my miserable nothingness before my eyes...! I often take a little passage for my meditation..... Oh, how poor and sinful I then feel....! The *Imitation of Christ* is a clear mirror for me shedding light into my poor soul and letting me see my failures clearly..! Take up your cross and follow me!!! These words with which the dear Saviour invites me to follow Him are the foundation stone of my heart in which the cross is set, – and with love and gratitude I want to greet it and with love of the cross and gratitude for the cross shall I the draw the last breath of my life. I see my sickbed as a quiet monastery cell in which I can truly observe the three holy religious vows. And if I cannot bodily follow a religious vocation (which was my most ardent wish) in my spirit I can live a quiet, hidden monastic life. O my Lord and God, since You Yourself know my heart better than I can even imagine, in total love I offer You myself with all my weakness; this is the only thing (failings and imperfections) that I believe I possess in abundance. I could not report anything beautiful and good about myself, because my wretchedness and weakness in all virtues is always clearly before my eyes; – and yet I am so happy; – because my heaven on earth is the God of love and grace who comes into my heart each day in Holy Communion and makes it a heavenly kingdom in miniature, that is, the heaven of suffering in union with Him. My heaven in suffering often allows me to see sublime things in spirit, – and as a return gift to my holy Bridegroom, I want to offer Him my life in love and suffering, until the wonderful day when I pass away to eternal union in Heaven! My motto is: suffering, love, expiation!

O Jesus, in Holy Communion and on the cross have I learned to love You.

O holy peace of the grave, for which my tired heart longs..! Only on the other side of the grave will my happiness be full and my longing satisfied, that is, my longing for Jesus alone..! Often in spirit I wander through the cemetery and greet all the silent sleepers, asking them also to pray for wretched me, when I shall be so fortunate to take my place among them, like a little grain of wheat, ready for the great seed-sowing of eternity...!

Each Holy Communion is another gemstone for the eternal crown..!

Gladly will I bear the cross and pain – It brings me after death to heaven!

Most Sacred Heart of Jesus, be Thou the longing of my poor heart. No suffering is too difficult in order to reach heaven and a life of suffering is too small a price to pay to look for a moment in God's eyes. O beautiful spring-like day that never ends, when will you dawn and lead me to the eternally bright heights...!

Longing for heaven can be satisfied here below only with Holy Communion, the inner union with Jesus ...! This is already each time an anticipation of the everlasting banquet. Holy Communion is my heaven on earth, – it is my heaven in suffering, – it is my heaven in total self-offering to Him whom I love and who dwells in my soul. I want to suffer and die only for love. United with Him I will embrace my little cross daily with love and desire, until I hear the call: Let us go to the house of the Lord ....!

I have three keys to heaven: The largest is made of raw iron and is heavy in weight: that is my suffering!
The second is my needle....
The third is my pen...!
With all these keys I will work hard each day to open heaven's gate, and each key shall be embellished with three crosses and three crowns: prayer, penance and self-denial!

One learns even in terrible pain, – to love suffering and to smile ..!

Today I can see the three places in the hereafter, – and tomorrow I can already be in one of the three!

O Lord, let my heart be stolen by your Heart, burning with love, in such a way that in the future it is no longer in me, – but dwelling in an indivisible union of love in You and have mercy on me, a poor sinner.

Most Sacred Heart of Jesus, all my trust is in You and in suffering and joy shall my tongue praise Your name, now, and with all the angels and chosen ones throughout all eternity.

Every Holy Communion is for me a new elevation to the throne of the Most Sacred Heart....! During every Holy Communion I feel as if my heart loses itself in God my Saviour; and even in sleep I often see the sacred Host in my dreams; – one moment it floats before my eyes, to look into the eyes of my heavenly Bridegroom, – the next moment I myself am before the Tabernacle, etc. In my dream I can pray so much more devoutly, ... than when I am awake...!

Years ago I also received a spiritual Communion in the morning upon awakening – and before and after every period of devotion; and for a few years now spiritual Communion is my 15-minute nourishment for my soul ...! Through a frequent reception of spiritual Communion the soul becomes strong and all those great weaknesses of the soul disappear, – so that a person can always be recollected at work and everywhere. Through spiritual Communion the fire of love is always burning in our heart and it is well-lighted, because in Holy Communion the dear Saviour comes to dwell in our heart..!

My God, my heart rejoices in You since that first holy hour of grace of my life, since my first holy banquet, at which my heart was full and totally satisfied in the purest happiness of Your beatific grace, since I was able to rest for the first time on Your holy Heart...! O unforgettable, holy hour...! You know, O my

Jesus, what first-fruits I offered you then ...! I thank You also for that beautiful dream I had then, when in my dream you told me that my whole life would be a quiet, hidden life on the cross, and that I would blossom, like a passion flower, at the foot of your holy cross; – quietly hidden here, – and radiant above with You in eternity. O my God, even now at Holy Communion, it is still like this... as soon as the Holy Communion is in my heart, it seems to me that I completely lose myself in Jesus, – as if Jesus takes my heart away with Himself...! By day and by night my thoughts remain unceasingly with Him whom I love and who often by day or night, when I receive spiritual Communion, steals my heart away and frequently after an hour filled with the most blessed vision, I recall that I am still in this wretched world!

I want to be pleasing to God, – so I must renounce myself!

Everything has an end – only eternity has no end!

Lord, humble me and exalt Yourself!

I choose the Holy Spirit as my only comforter and protector in all things. May He be my advocate and the one who overcomes all my failings; and most of all He is the one who teaches me to prepare and offer things after Holy Communion..!

In each of the Lord's wounds, I place a special intention, – a special suffering.

If the dear God wants something, – any resistance is fruitless...!

Your hidden face, O my Jesus, is my heavenly Kingdom..!

Oh, we cannot value the great love of the dear Saviour enough. Day and night His divine heart, burning with love, rests on our heart and invites us to the heavenly banquet.

How gladly I would suffer martyrdom, if only my dear Jesus in the Blessed Sacrament would be better known and loved and many more souls would be on fire with longing for the highest good. I have no other desire on earth than to be consumed in the fire of Your Most Sacred Heart..! I would like to be totally dead to the world but often after a few hours I realize that I am still in this valley of tears. I would find no attraction in it, neither gold nor riches, – neither prestige nor honour, etc. My happiness, my joy and bliss is: Jesus alone, whom I love and who dwells in my soul.

Very often in my dreams I am allowed to receive Holy Communion; at those times I am able to pray more fervently than when I am awake ...!

The desire to possess God forever increases in me year after year ...., and when my heart shall be consumed by this blessed longing, then I may gently fall asleep on the heart of our holy God.

The fire of suffering – prepares for me the way to heavenly joy!

Oh – how good is the dear God, he gives me suffering, which is so necessary for me to draw nearer to him. O my Jesus, I place everything in Your Most Sacred Heart, – replace everything that is lacking and still filled with error. O my Jesus, I unite the pains that I now suffer with Your suffering and I want to gladly beaer them in penance for my sins. I want to spend all my days of suffering in a spirit of penance and reparation and love in union with God's holy will.

Each day I also want to thank the dear God for all the graces and favours. And thus I am always happy and when I must suffer very much, I am still happier and whatever costs me more effort, in knitting or writing, or in whatever I do, I shall do it with special liking and pay no attention to the strain; rather, I am happy if I can through some kind of work or my poor lines of writing make give joy to another. And so I do so, wherever I am! One must first of all seek the good Lord in every place and encourage others for Him...., and we ourselves must forsake ourselves entirely...., so that the Lord can work and reign unhindered in our heart..! And so I do this with all of God's gifts. If, for example, at night I look at the starry heavens, I ask the stars to greet the dear Lord with their light. I often say: O you dear little star who adorn your Jesus, my Beloved, tell Him, – that I am sick– and that longing for Him makes my heart beat in an unusual way ...!

My Heart is still penetrated entirely by Him – Whom I love – and Who is hidden in the sacred Host, who became nourishment for my soul..!

My wish and my intention is: to help save a great company of souls and draw them to heaven.

I would like to help foster the interests of Jesus everywhere, by good example and the like, – or through prayer, sacrifice and suffering.

The first item on my agenda is: no more sins! Those three short words are all that I have set for my goal in the course of the day. And when I make my examination of conscience in the evening..., I feel so happy if I can say of the whole day: I was always in God's presence! That is, my spirit rests in God's Heart! With all my wretchedness, sins and errors, the dear God does not hesitate to dwell in me, a poor sinner. Praised be the Most Holy Trinity always and forever. The thought that Jesus, my Beloved, dwells in me always makes me so happy in suffering and unpleasantries, and immense is the happiness I feel after Holy Communion in the persence of the dear Saviour..., or to put it better, whether I feel suffering or joy, I always feel the Lord's presence.

O Holy Spirit of love and grace, You are always the ruler of my poor heart; banish everything that You do not want from my heart and protect it here and in eternity, as Your temple consecrated to You, – so that Jesus my Beloved can look upon my poor heart rejoicing in its redemption, – and the heavenly Father in its creation.

Oh how blessed is a person who can daily participate in the banquet of love… and can daily savour the bread of angels. Oh what inner joy and happiness one feels at all times whenever he can say: Today I was fortunate to be able to receive the dear Saviour in Holy Communion into my poor heart…. and tomorrow I shall have this same good fortune again…! Whenever one lives day by day in union with the dear Saviour and thinking… how we can give Him joy in the course of the day, etc, … oh how blessed is this life with Him.

I have often experienced that on those days when the world is at its craziest, and the dear God is even more offended, as when there are balls and such and all night long revelry is indulged in, that I must suffer much more than usual and I cannot make anyone understand how hard these hours of suffering are for me, and I can only say: I am awash in suffering and pain. My God, may Your holy will be done in me, poor sinner, at all times. Everything for love of You; for Your consolation and for reparation to You. O Jesus who suffered scourging, may the stripes of Your passion crush everything that is physical, that is purely natural in me, – only if the soul profits from bodily privation, – and earthly death is followed by eternal resurrection.

How beautiful is contemplation with Jesus.

I often hasten to offer every little sacrifice out of love to the Lord. I accept with great love all the little and insignificant things and never think about achieving great things; only the small and childlike things that happen in the course of the day, things that demand a small sacrifice, I place with the greatest love that I, a poor sinner can, in the hands of the dear Saviour. I often think that the dear Saviour is also pleased by many little flowers.

My last earthly wish, one I always had in the first years of my illness, is that I be allowed to die before my dear mother does; this desire, too, I offered to the Lord in Holy Communion, so that my will can totally die, – let me bear suffering and pain according to Your will, – let me suffer on the cross which You have prepared for me, – until I am dear and pleasing to You. I eagerly accept the chalice of bitterness and thank You until my last breath.

In the beautiful month of May, I want to change my clothes, i.e., I want to throw off my garments of sin, and peel away what is earthly, selfish, egotistical and self-centred, and I want to put on the mantle of the dear Mother of God with all her virtues and meditate each day on her holy life. Each day I will weave a crown of multi-coloured flowers and try to bind to each of them one or the other of the beautiful virtues of the dear Mother of God. O dear, good Mother, in your hands I place each day this crown of flowers and ask you to present it to the dear Saviour. However, in order to find such beautiful flowers, we must descend each day further into the valley of humility! There we will find before us many paths, many dark ravines, where we must make great effort to pass through, especially when it is really dry in the garden of the soul,... and also quite dark...! Greater caution is needed when there are more shadows in the garden of the soul, – in order not to miss the sunny areas where we can find the flowers with which we can give joy to Jesus, our Beloved. Oh – how beautiful is such a life, – when all a person seeks is flowers, ––– flowers to gladden God's eyes, ––– flowers, to console the Most Sacred Heart of Jesus and Mary, ––– flowers that remove the thorns that evil people have driven into Most Sacred Heart of Jesus and his mother..! Our life shall be a floral wreath. Oh twice happy when our floral wreath is already green and flowering when we return to the Father's house. It is a great consolation and joy for me when I look back, and I see that I have always venerated the dear mother of God. Oh what happy hours I recall....!

For an awfully long time I have no more will of my own, only the will of God has been enthroned as the single ruler of my heart and Him alone, – Whom I love and Who daily visits my poor heart in Holy Communion again, – to Him alone, – have I totally dedicated myself without a will, (so that I have no will, no self-will of my own). Do with me what You will, O divine Saviour, I want to suffer for You, suffer and die with You. And this is what I do with everything, from A – Z.

The cross and suffering is my ladder to heaven and how comforting it is to be able to suffer under God's gaze and united with Him! How subline is such a day of suffering! Whenever I have a day of particularly bad pain, I quietly thank the dear

God in the quiet of my heart and often think to myself: Well, now, my soul, today you had another day of especially great suffering and so you have had a resemblance with Jesus alone. If I have a particularly bad headache, – O dearest Jesus, then I think to myself: you have let me experience a tiny bit of your crown of thorns. If I suffer severe pain in my back, I thank you, O dear Jesus, for allowing me to experience the bed of your hard cross. If if may suffer something throughout my whole body, especially because of my many wounds, I thank You, my Lord and God, that I can have a little experience of the terrible scourging that Your most holy body had to suffer for me, a poor sinner. And when the night is as painful and sleepless as the day, I can contemplate Jesus's death on the cross and I exclaim: How easy it is to die with Jesus on the cross, – if one has lived with Jesus on the cross!

My thoughts and intentions
for the 12 months.

January:

With Mary, my dear and good Mother, I consecrate myself to You, dear Jesus; – in her – and united with her, with her immaculate heart, – I want to live a hidden life!

February:

O Mother of Sorrows, united with you, – I want to climb the mountain of pain and sorrow and you can place me on the altar as an offering for sins, – so that with your help I can make some reparation to the Crucified Saviour, – for the many sins and heinous deeds of the godless!

March:

Most holy, immaculate Virgin, united with you I entrust myself to the intercession of your holy spouse, St. Joseph, – oh, hand my poor soul over to him, so that with you he can lead me to my eternal goal, – to Jesus alone!

April:

Oh Mother of Sorrows, lead me up Mount Calvary! May your suffering, – may your repulsion for sin be passed on to me! – Teach me to recognize the cross, ... the mortal agony.... Jesus' love... and our ingratitude.... and give me always a burning thirst to work for the salvation of immortal souls, – to pray and suffer for them and that I can always spend my days in the love of the Eucharistic Heart of Jesus!

May:

O holy Queen of May, I consecrate to you and give you all the energy of my soul. – Help me to pray, – and remove from my memory every thought – that does not regard Jesus and you alone. Teach me to say from the depths of my heart: I am the handmaid of the Lord!'

June:

O dear, good Mother, may you give and consecrate me to the Heart of Jesus, burning with love. – Help me to prepare my poor heart and lend me your heart, – when I receive Holy Communion. Help me to adore my dear Jesus and thank Him also for me! – Defend Jesus in my heart and let Him live in me, – grow in me – act and reign in me. – Oh, extend His Kingdom in the hearts of others and fortify it ever more.

July:

O spotless lily of the Most Holy Trinity, united with you, I want to gather in spirit the precious Blood that dear Jesus shed on his path of martyrdom, in order to place it on the altar of sacrifice of His Most Sacred Heart. In spirit I want to fall down and adore that precious Blood, – which in so many Holy Communions has been drunk unworthily and dishonoured.

August:

O most holy heart of Mary, take me under the mantle of your protection and teach me to love – suffer – die, in order at your side to see that glorious day, – in which united with you I may adore dear Jesus forever and ever.

September:

Holy mother of God, together with my guardian angel and the nine choirs of angels and all the saintly spirits, lead me always to the tabernacle, – to Jesus the Bridegroom of my soul; and to your prayer of adoration and that of the holy angels I unite my feeble praise and united with them, I cry: Holy, holy, holy..!

October:

Queen of the Holy Rosary, I am entirely yours forever, lead me united with you and Saint Francis through this valley of tears, – with Saint Francis following also in the school of the cross and suffering. May your purity, your fidelity eradicate in us, O good mother, the least little imperfection and increase our love for the supreme good.

November:

O holy Mother of Sorrows and mother of all the suffering souls in Purgatory, – ask for me true penance and an improvement of my life. I hand over to you my heart and help me to be faithful to my intention: No more sins!'

December:

O holy, Immaculate Conception, place my dear Jesus in my heart in Holy Communion and ask for me perseverance to the end. My only desire is: Jesus and Mary!

~

"Give honours and crowns to whom You will, O Lord, here on earth – For me reserve no other crown than your own crown of thorns!"

Heavenly Father, I offer You, through the hands of my dear heavenly mother, the Most Holy Body and Most Precious Blood of Your divine Son, for all those who will die today – as many times over as the Holy Mass will be celebrated throughout the world from this moment until tomorrow morning!'

Prayer to my Guardian Angel:[14]

O my dear holy angel – the bell for Mass is sounding –

How I would love to hasten to Church – But my illness keeps me away –

Therefore I ask you to participate – In my place, I pray –

Full of honour bring Jesus – My offering of thanksgiving and love –

During the Offertory, tell Him – That I offer Him my heart –

And that I am quite prepared – To suffer for Him for all eternity–

Place my heart and all I am – As an offering to Jesus Christ –

At the time of Consecration – Help me to pray fervently –

My Lord and God, silently I implore You – When I see the Sacred Host –

Lamb of God, with your precious blood – Quench the fires of souls–

And at Holy Communion – Receive for me the Son of God –

Tell Him – how much my heart longs – In humility, love and reparation –

14 In the original, the prayer is composed of lines of verse written in iambic tetrameter, with the first part of the line rhyming with the end of the same line.

At Holy Communion – Ask Him for countless graces for me –

Help me to keep my heart pure – Whenever Jesus comes to me –

Present it to Him as a little blossom – That it may bloom upon the altar –

For as long as he wants in this world – And also there in eternity –

Bring me the holy blessing – Dear little angel, I thank you –

Be near me in my suffering – Until I am with you in heaven!'

~

My holy guardian angel, take me in spirit to participate in this most holy Eucharistic Sacrifice.

In the holy Mass I unite my feeble prayer to the offering of the priest on the altar.

Heavenly Father, I offer You through the hands of the priest Your dear Son with that love– with that love with which he offered Himself for us poor sinners on the cross.

While the holy Mass is being celebrated, it seems that I am on Mount Calvary and there I see in spirit all the scenes of the passion of our dear Saviour. And while I pray along with the

Mass prayers, or the holy Rosary.... I experience in that holy time of grace a great bliss, especially in the three main parts of the holy Mass. Then I pray very much for the conversion of sinners!

O dearest Jesus, through the most worthy presence of your holy and unblemished Body and precious Blood, I ask You to give me the conversion of those sinners .....!

I offer You, and through You to the Most Holy Trinity, everything that You do on this altar ...!

Eternal Father, I offer You Your dear Son, I offer You His life, His bitter suffering, His painful death....! I offer You the suffering of Your Sorrowful Mother ......! Grant me, a poor sinner, grace and mercy..!

My Lord and God, I adore You from the bottom of my poor nothigness and ask You through your Most Precious Blood, that you poured out for all; give a drop of Your most holy and precious Blood for my poor soul, a drop for my parents and siblings and my siblings'children, – for the Reverend pastor, for the whole parish, – for all my benefactors, friends and foes – for all the priests of the holy Church, – for the Holy Father, – for all the Bishops and Cardinals – for every soul .... for whom I have promised to pray...! for the ..... for whom I offer my suffering, – for the souls of all children of our homeland, – for the souls of all sinners – for every single soul in our cemetery, – for every single soul in Purgatory.

My Lord and my God, I close myself up in Your Most Sacred Heart, with the innermost desire: Oh satisfy my desire,– You, the Bridegroom of my soul – to receive in spirit You, the true sacrificial Lamb ....!

Most Sacred Heart of Jesus I trust in You! My God, I thank You!

Ich want to accompany the dear Saviour, not only up to Palm Sunday – where He was greeted with great rejoicing by the throngs as He entered Jerusalem; but to the great message that He spoke on the cross: It is finished.

However, when the great Holy Week came and Jesus began, so fruitfully for us to suffer, – all those who had welcomed Him before, stayed at a distance, – except for the few who remained faithful.

If we practice daily with the splinters of the cross, – then we also learn to bear with greater steadfastness and courage, – when after Palm Sunday the dear Saviour sends us – a greeting from the cross.

Whenever I do my daily tasks as if I were climbing to another level of humiliation, etc. I have in my heart a quiet joy....! Because whatever often costs me great sacrifice, – brings me also the greatest merit. The more I climb down with my own ego to gather flowers in the valley of humility, – the freer and higher my soul soars to Jesus ..! O with how many treasures I can adorn my eternal "Home". O dear heavenly mother, if these sufferings that I now endure could be a consolation for you, – Oh please give them to Jesus and console Him...! Every day I want to become smaller in my dust.

Jesus says: Forsake yourself – and you will find me!
Lord, I gladly surrender myself totally to you.

My wish for myself and all mankind is to rest in the shadow of the cross, on which love is raised up, so that our hearts remain there irreproachably and fulfill their duties.

What I am now suffering, – I must tell myself – regardless of what it is and what it's called, – that everything comes from God

The dear God could in an instant take everything away from me, but no, – it is so useful to me..! And in holy love and joy I want to embrace and kiss my cross and, according to God's holy will, suffer until I am ripe for eternal love, for eternal life. O my God, I praise You more for all the suffering that you give me than for all the many unending joys I have received from You.

One does not achieve true divine love without drinking from the chalice of suffering, – without having borne the loss of light, – and abandonment by God.

In the school of the cross, every hour there are lessons in will-power and in mortification of one's own desires!

Lord, take me as I am, including all my defects, and make me how You want me to be.

If we could often see the picture of our soul, I think, we would see so many icebergs in it, that is, in the hours of abandonment and in the hours of darkness, etc., when the divine Sun with his warming rays withdraws...! But how useful is this for us! What great merit we could draw from this! The greater is the longing for Jesus our Beloved, – the faster the ice melts, – the quicker the darkness fades. One cross after another – one pain after another – one abandonment after another, everything, everything I accept in joy, whatever Your hand offers me, O my God.

My suffering has lasted for more than 21 years. Daily I experience to some degree the nails of the cross and the points of the crown of thorns. Yet I am so happy and thank the dear Saviour for every thorn of suffering.The way of the cross that I have traveled, tells me clearly that the dear God has shown me so many graces. After such a long, difficult suffering, it is the Lord's will that I by his grace am still living; – I live on the cross, – and I also hope, – to finish happily through and with the cross – and the Lord will be gracious and merciful to me. The song of praise of the three young men in the fiery furnace is also an important part of my routine, and I want to cry out with them: Everything, everything praise and exalt the Lord ...!

May every moment of my life and suffering be spent in doing God's will and in praising Him, and I will rejoice, when the number of my days of suffering is complete, to go to Jesus forever.

I think to myself: My bed is God's will, and I lie here now as if I am nailed to God's will. Everything that I must suffer in my condition I lovingly accept from God's hand and so I hope that God's holy will and my wretchedness are one.

When one is united daily with Jesus in Holy Communion, illness is not so hard..!

And if whole mountains of suffering surround me, I trust in Jesus, – and with all the more fervour I call out to Him: Most Sacred Heart of Jesus I trust in You..! I keep myself as much as possible in a spirit of recollection, – so that, when I have to speak with someone, – I think of Jesus... and I recall His presence in love, thanksgiving, expiation and adoration. Often whenever there is someone with me, my spirit converses with Jesus amid many interruptions..., indeed even in sleep, i.e., in my dreams, I often experience great recollection in prayer. At night, too, as I lie awake sleeplessly for many hours, I am always in a spirit of recollection; – during the day, too, I experience great joy....! Always and everywhere my thought, desire and will are always turned towards Jesus. Neither in the noise of distraction nor in the din of suffering or the tumult of worldly cares and excitement will we manage to hear the dear Saviour's intimations, – but only when we make the effort to think of His presence. Let us keep everything else far away from our heart, – so that we can hear the inspirations from

Jesus. Let us remain little in our own eyes, by means of simplicity, obedience and devotion.

'We should be like the snail, who carries his house on his back, – but whenever his feelers encounter a hostile object, he immediately withdraws. Thus we should not always be directed towards externals, but dedicate ourselve as much as possible to inner recollection. What advantage would it be to us if we seldom inhabit the cottage of our soul, – how can we hear the voice of the Holy Spirit? If we hear only the voices of creatures? If we are so seldom at home and we leave our heavenly Guest alone, – how can we be conscious of His nearness and His presence?

There are many flowers that no one has ever seen and gathered, namely Alpine roses and edelweiss. They bloom, – they die, – and no eye has seen them, but God's alone. As many flowers as there are, – so many virtues are there as well. How often a hidden life is like, – a flower that has never been seen, – and yet our Father in Heaven sees it. How many a quiet virgin does not traffic with the world, – remains hidden from its eyes, – living only for the great Alone – for Whom – all the flowers bloom, and sees in every little flower the eye of God, – and every little flower, reminds her to imitate the holy virtues. No human eye sees it, – what such a hidden soul gains for heaven, – no one sees it but the eye of God, – she is a silently hidden flower for heaven. Oh how I would like to cry out to all the virgins: How beautiful is chastity among all the virtues – how beautiful is the heart's garden of a virgin decorated with so many flowers with such a beautiful perfume. The Bridegroom of pure souls would gladly live there, and the holy angels rejoice over such flowers, that are their playmates. I would like to call out to every single virgin: maiden, protect your innocence at any cost! Save your immortal soul, and let the springtime of your heart bloom in you with its fragrant perfume, – the whole year through, until the Lord transplants you into the eternal meadows, – where all, – of pure heart shall see God. The virgins shall be near the Lord – here and in heaven.

Most Sacred Heart of Jesus I trust in You – I shall not be discredited in eternity. My place of refuge is: Jesus in the Most Holy Sacrament. You, O my Saviour, have the words of eternal life. When we are weak, You strengthen us with the Holy Banquet; – when we weep, You are our consolation, etc. You calm the storms of life that rage within us and around us, and perfect peace reigns. Only for You, O my God, do I yearn...! Oh when will I be able to say: My Beloved is mine and I am His, – I live no longer, not I, but Jesus lives in me!'

'Everything for the greater glory of God! Everything with God and under the protection of the ever-blessed Virgin and Saint Joseph!'
May the mercy of our holy God triumph from age to age!

"The Sun of my life is Jesus in the Most Holy Sacrament ...! And even if I have to suffer much, – isn't every day of suffering, and every hour of suffering, enlightened by this heavenly Sun? Whenever I think to myself, e.g., things are going badly for me, because perhaps I have to suffer this or that, etc., – and thus think that I cannot, – that would certainly hurt the dear Saviour and I do not want to harbour such thoughts in my heart...! And furthermore, when one is sick for such a long time, one learns also to love suffering, and to smile in the deepest pain. It also helps very much that I often think about the great mystery of Jesus in Holy Communion, so that I can accept everything joyfully. Oh how I shall rejoice, when the feast of eternal union begins ....! Each day when the hour strikes that Jesus instituted the Most Blessed Sacrament and another 12 hours separates me from my morning Communion, – I make a little act of thanksgiving for today and then offer offer everything up in preparation for the next day's Holy Communion, ... everything I shall do and suffer until the following day...! I unite my modest actions to the countless great virtues, which so many souls throughout the whole world are preparing this evening and throughout the night for Jesus...., and which the saints already performed during their earthly life. In the various prayers, etc. I always ask the Holy Spirit for love and grace, – it is his task to bring my poor soul in the right state for the worthy reception of Holy Communion. A lot depends on the right state of soul! O my God, grant me this grace and also many sacrifices and much love of the cross and a courageous ascent to the Father's house. – Ever forward, – always following the cross, – always upwards to Jesus...!

'Passion, cross and death of Jesus, – Be my consolation in all my want!'
'The Kingdom of Heaven suffers violence, – and only the violent shall possess it!'

'Wherever Jesus is, everything goes well and nothing is difficult, – where Jesus is not, countless tribulation and trouble hold sway! Praised be [15] Jesus in Holy Communion!

Two requests that are very close to my heart, I place especially before the Sacred Heart of Jesus after Holy Communion and devoutly ask Him in His love and grace to grant them to me. First, that He may wipe out the sins I have not yet committed and the punishment for all my sins, so that free from the oppression of any spiritual guilt, with a joyful heart I may walk the way of the divine commandments and gather up treasure for eternal life. Secondly, may Jesus give me the grace, through the power of this heavenly meal, – never again – to commit a conscious sin.... and from day to day to avoid and eliminate my many unconscious errors and imperfections. In all of these points I want to do my best to give the dear God joy. What precious minutes my dear Jesus gives me when He comes in Holy Communion! These minutes are thus a time of enrichment with treasure that neither rust nor moth can destroy, – a time of spiritual harvest.., as if there were no more. When during the night, or even by day I do not manage to pray well, in the meantime I just take many spiritual breaths; (that's what I call my little ejaculatory prayers.) In these little prayers

15 The German expression, *"Es lebe"* is best rendered as Viva in Romance languages and/or "Hooray", "Hoorah", "Three cheers for " or "Long live..." in English. None of these seem appropriate, so here it has been translated as "Praised be"

there is a great treasure....., they prepare for me the golden road to the dear Saviour in the Most Holy Sacrament .... and like a powerful magnet, draw me to Jesus ... whenever I go in spirit to visit the dear Saviour in the Most Holy Sacrament, I go to Him by menas of so many little prayers.... Oh these beautiful golden roads..! That is how I always do it...!

O my God I want to lovingly accept the cross that You offer me.How could I struggle against it? No, my Jesus, I promised You when I dedicated myself as an offering for souls, that I want to accept from Your hand every cross that You see fit to send me. Shall I not also rejoice when day after day you place a cross upon my shoulders and thereby give me an opportunity to make reparation to Your divine Heart for sins? O my Jesus, I want to embrace this little cross lovingly and unto my last breath may it be my joy, my glory and my delight. I want to be totally dead to the world and not glory in anything except the cross of Jesus, my divine Bridegroom, through Whom the world is crucified to me and I to the world. I long for no treasure other than holy poverty, no other delight than His suffering, no other love than He Himself. It matters not to me what others do, think or say, – in truth I am only what I am in God's eyes. We can never think too humbly of ourselves; we must come to the point that in the eyes of others we are quite imperfect, rather than give in to our self-love whenever an opportunity for self-humiliation presents itself. O my God, You alone know how poor, wretched and imperfect I am in Your holy eyes; be gracious and merciful to me, a poor sinner.

'The poorest person of all is – the one who lives without Jesus; – but the richest of all is the one who is united daily with Jesus in Holy Communion and remains His friend!'

Jesus alone, – is the object of my thoughts, words and actions and the center of all the drives and feelings of my heart. O dearest Jesus, – when I work, be my intention, – when I suffer, my consolation, – when I rest, my relaxation, – when I wake, my attention, – when I sleep, my dream.

O my Jesus, when you release me from my earthly bonds, let me enjoy forever that bliss that you let me feel after Holy Communion...!

I have often thought, when in spirit I prayed before the blessed Sacrament, – that Holy Communion is called the "Bread of Angels"; – and we poor pilgrims on earth can be nourished daily with the Bread of Angels ...! Oh, shouldn't we then live like angels..., with more ardent worship and burning longing prepare our poor heart daily and keep it pure for Jesus alone...! The best preparation and thanksgiving is a holy life, so that we can always say: I live no longer, not I, – but Jesus lives in me ..!

Daily offering of my 12 hours of reparation before the Most Blessed Sacrament!

1. O heavenly Father, I offer You these hours, to expiate for all the iniquity and ignominy heaped upon the Most Sacred Eucharistic Heart of Jesus and especially to adore the Precious Blood in the lonely hours of the night, when so many sins are committed.

2. To receive, through Mary, my dear and good Mother, the graces, that today at least one moral sin shall be prevented.

3. To implore grace and mercy, especially for those sinners, who are near the abyss and the grace they most need: Most Sacred Heart of Jesus, give me many souls, who can hardly keep themselves from despair and grant them a happy death.

4. To make reparation to the Eucharistic Heart of Jesus, for all the unworthy receptions of Holy Communion....!

5. To implore grace, blessings and mercy, for all the living priests, for the preservation of the holiness of their vocation; so that they may lead many souls to dear Jesus.

6. For all the souls of priests in Purgatory!

7. For all the poor souls in Purgatory!

8. For those benefactors, whom I include daily in my feeble prayer.... and for whom I have offered my suffering...!

9. For the Holy Father and all members of the holy Catholic Church!

10. For all missionaries in foreign pagan lands!

11. For my parents, siblings, relatives, friends and benefactors.

12. For the grace of a happy death and the worthy reception of the Last Sacraments. Praised be the Most Sacred Heart of Jesus and the precious Blood in the Most Holy Sacrament of the altar.

Honour be to the dear God alone – success to those who work in the Lord's vineyard – and for myself, only the cross and suffering, if the Lord deigns to send me such!

I would rather die, – than deliberately offend the dear God with a lie!

Evening Examination of Conscience!

Have I consciously and faithfully adhered to my daily schedule and agenda....?

Was I often recollected in God's presence and did I accept everything that happened throughout the day, whether suffering or joy, gratefully from God's hand ....?

Did I completely deny my self-will and did I always live, suffer, etc., according to God's holy will....?

Did I mortify my senses in everything.....?

Have I denied myself.....?

Have I always preferred my neighbour's well-being over my own .....?

Have I always considered myself the lowliest dust and the poorest sinner.....?

O my God be gracious and merciful to my poor soul. Repentance out of love.....!

My holy guardian angel, n. D. m. V. v. g. T. a. and bring it into the presence of our holy God.........!

I want to do everything in the presence of Jesus ...!
When I wake, – may it be under Jesus' watchful eyes....!
When I sleep, – may I dream of Jesus ....!
When I work, – Jesus is my Master ....!
When I write, – Jesus guides my pen...!
When I pray, – Jesus shall form and enliven my words..!
When I am tired, – Jesus is my rest....!
When I am hungry or thirsty, – Jesus becomes my food and drink...!
When I am sick and suffering greatly, – Jesus is be my love and physician....!
When I die, I will die in Jesus...!
Jesus, – shall be the last word on my dying lips....!
Jesus, – shall close my eyes...!
May the heart of Jesus be my sepulchre...!
My God I thank You! My God I love you!'

[Praised be Jesus[16] in Holy Communion, these holy moments...... and how much I would like to still say about Jesus, but I simply cannot do it.... I find neither the words nor any other way of making myself understood; I would just like to say that in these moments I am immersed in an unspeakable bliss. Once the dear Saviour said to me from the Tenth Station and from an ejaculatory prayer, "My Jesus mercy!"][17]

16 See footnote n. 15 above.
17 This addendum in italics can be found in a transcription of the *Thoughts and Memories of Anna Schäffer*, in BKR Abt. CAS K 16, AS 19, cf. Introduction.

Abbreviations

Abt.	=	Abteilung Selig- and Heiligsprechungsprozesse (Department for Beatification and Canonisation Processes)
BKR	=	Bischöfliches Konsistorium Regensburg (Diocesan Consistory of Regensburg)
CAS	=	Causa Anna Schäffer (Cause of Canonisation of Anna Schäffer)
D.	=	Document
K	=	Karton (Carton)
Proc.	=	Process

Index

Anna Schäffer from Mindelstetten (1882 – 1925)

Biographical sketch

Anna Schäffer was born on 18 February 1882, the daughter of a blacksmith from Mindelstetten (Diocese of Regensburg). When in 1894 she was allowed to make her First Holy Communion, she offered her life as an offering to Christ. At the age of 13 she came to Regensburg to perform domestic work. She hoped to be able to earn the dowry needed to enter a religious order; she wanted to be a missionary. After her father's death in 1896 she worked in Landshut.There in June 1898 she received her decisive vocation from Jesus: she would soon suffer much and for a long time. On 4 February 1901 her time of suffering did begin in the laundry of the forester's lodge at Stammham. The stovepipe over the boiler had worked loose from the wall, and she attempted to repair the damage. However, she slipped and fell into the hot lye, with both legs immersed above the knee. Neither in the hospital in Kösching, where she was first taken, nor in the clinic in Erlangen were they able to cure her wounds. After she was discharged in May 1902 as an invalid, her condition continuously deteriorated, so that soon she was confined to bed. Her severe infirmity was also accompanied by bitter poverty. After a period of understandable rebellion, Anna learned in the hard school of suffering to recognize God's will and to accept it joyfully. In suffering and poverty the young woman discerned a loving call from the Crucified, her life's offering and fulfilment. She decided to offer her life and suffering to God as an atonement for sin and developed – strengthened by Holy Communion – an astonishing love for prayer, penance and expiation. Anna promised her prayers and in speech and writing consoled those who turned to her. On the morning of 5 October 1925 the dying woman received for the last time her Eucharistic Lord, the source of strength for her 25-years of suffering. Since her death Anna's tomb has been the destination of countless people who appeal to her intercession in need and distress or thank her for the help she has shown them. Anna Schäffer was raised up by God as a shining sign of his love. She harmoniously combined the apostolate of action with the apostolate of prayer and suffering, of offering and expiation. In this is her greatness and her meaning. Pope Benedict XVI has announced that she will be canonised on 21 October 2012.

Extract from the original manuscript

Gedanken u. Erinnerungen meines Krankenlebens – u. meine Sehnsucht nach der ewigen Heimat!

Gott allein, Gott allein genügt!

„Nimm Dein Kreuz auf dich u. folge mir nach!" Diese Worte aus der Nachfolge Christi, mit denen mich der lb. Heiland einladet Ihm nachzufolgen, sind mir die Grundsteine meines Herzens auf welchem das Kreuz aufgestellt ist. Mit Liebe u. Dankbarkeit, will ich es jeden Augenblick begrüßen, – u. in Kreuzesliebe u. Kreuzesdank, soll der letzte Hauch meines Lebens verwehen!

„Am Kreuze, – u. in der hl. Kommunion, o mein Herr u. Gott, habe ich dich lieben gelernt!"

Der Wille u. die Fülle des Glaubens, muß das Kreuz in unserem Leben allzeit lebendig bilden u. machen, – so daß jedes von sich selbst sagen kann: – Ich lebe, – doch nicht ich – sondern Jesus der Kreuztragende lebt in mir u. mit Ihm gehe ich: dem Kreuze nach!"

„Das Ziel meines Kreuzes ist: Kalvarias Höhe! Auf diese Höhe will ich blicken, wenn in den Schmerzensstunden meines Lebens, mein Leib von Schmerzen durchwühlt wird. Jenes Licht, das mir von dieser Höhe zuströmt – läßt mir alles leicht u. licht erscheinen, – denn ich sehe ja mein Vorbild – meinen Heiland, wie viel Er für mich Unwürdige gelitten hat. Und vereint mit Ihm, den ich liebe u. der in meiner Seele wohnt, will ich gerne mein Kreuz umfassen u. Ihm folgen: dem Kreuze nach!"

Das Kreuz ist der Hammer – der die Unsterblichkeitskrone schmiedet, die wir im Himmel tragen werden, – wenn wir unser Kreuz mit Mut u. Ergebung auf Erden getragen haben.

Ich habe im Herzen stille heilige Freude, weil mich der Herr die Glut Seines Kreuzes inwendig verspüren läßt.

Das Kreuz ist mein Führer, – es ist meine Kraft, – es ist mein Licht, – es ist meine Hilfe, – es ist mein Schild, – es ist mein Trost, – es ist mein Leben, – es ist mein Ruhm, – es ist meine Ruhe u. es wird meine Belohnung sein!"

„Wenn wir auf Jesus am Kreuze schauen, – oder in seiner Liebe im Tabernakel betrachten, – so können wir alles mit Geduld ertragen!“

„Kreuz u. Leiden, – sind meine Erziehung für den Himmel!“
Der Weg zum Himmel – führt über via dolorosa nach Kalvaria, – u. erst von da weg, zu den ewigen Hallen!
Durch Kreuz u. Leiden, Trübsale u. Widerwärtigkeiten zieht uns der Herr hinauf zu seinem Kreuze, – hinauf zum Kalvarienberg. Nur wer Ihm auf den Kalvarienberg folgt – den läßt Er auch auf dem Berge seiner Seligkeit (?) steigen, – denn hinter den Leiden dieser Zeit, – liegt die Herrlichkeit Gottes. Überwindung führt hinan zum Kreuz, – zum Gipfel der Liebe – darum verleugnen wir uns selbst u. folgen wir dem Kreuze nach!“

Ich dürste o Herr nach Kreuz und Leiden u. verlange in diesem Tränentale keinen Tropfen des Trostes mehr! Unter dem Schatten des Kreuzes u. in der strahlenden Liebesglut vor dem Tabernakel, will ich die Tage meines Leidens verbringen. Jedes Tröpflein Blut im Herzen – jede heiße Glut der Schmerzen – jede tiefe Leidenswunde – jede süße Freudenstunde – Alles dir o Gott zu Ehren – hier und dort dein Lob zu mehren!“
Mir kommt oft vor lauter Schmerzen vor, ich sei in ein Dornengestrüpp verwickelt, u. ich machte mich dann wie jenes Schäflein, daß der gute Hirt im Dornengestrüpp fand. Ich habe dann im Herzen stille hl. Freude, denn dann weiß ich es ja, daß der Herr in meiner Nähe ist u. besonders in dieser hl. Fastenzeit da darf das Leiden schon schwerer sein u. ich fühle es auch ....! Hlst. Herz Jesu ich danke dir! Jedes Leidensröslein möchte ich meinem himml. Bräutigam an sein verwundetes Herz legen, – um Ihn zu trösten u. um Ihn zu erfreuen.
Ich freue mich so sehr, wenn ich einmal dieses Tränental verlassen darf. Nicht um des Leidens erlöst zu sein, möchte ich so gerne heim ....., sondern einzig nur .... Auch dort möchte ich nicht einen Augenblick untätig sein u. möchte gerne leiden bis zum Ende der Zeiten, bis alle Schäflein in den großen Schafstall eingegangen sein werden. Mein Wunsch ist, im Himmel durch mein fortwährendes Gebet, noch so manche Sünderseele retten zu können, was auch hier mein einziger Wunsch wäre. Für die Priester möchte ich aber jetzt u. auch dann das meiste beten, besonders für .... Denn durch das Wirken heiligmäßiger Priester können doch soviele Seelen gerettet, soviele Seelen zur Vollkommenheit gelangen.
Verbirg mich o gekreuzigte Liebe in die verwundete (?) Höhle deiner Seite, damit ich selig dort entschlafe u. am Schlummer deiner honigsüßen Liebe mich erquicke!“
O mein Gott ich liebe dich du ewige Schönheit, der du stets mein Herz mit dir verbindest (?), so oft ich an dich denke ...!